HEALING
RELATIONSHIPS
THROUGH FORGIVENESS

ACCEPTING GOD'S GRACE AND
GIVING IT TO OTHERS

A WORKBOOK COMPANION
FOR PERSONAL STUDY

DONALD E. JONES, PHD

J & A Book Publishers
www.jabookpublishers.com

ISBN-13: 978-0692737170
ISBN-10: 0692737170

DEDICATION

I dedicate this book to my Savior and Lord Jesus Christ. He has been with me every step of my journey upon the earth, and I so look forward to being in His presence forever and ever.

CONTENTS

ACKNOWLEDGMENTS

I want to thank my wonderful and gracious wife Carol who has supported me in this ministry with sacrifice, enthusiasm, encouragement, and accountability. Most of all, she has been a constant blessing because of her willingness to listen. I was always sharing with her the truths God had been teaching me as I studied His word and wrote this book. It consumed many hours. Thank you, Carol, and I deeply love you.

I want to thank my son Gregory R. Jones for volunteering to be the primary editor of this important book. Without his time and effort in painstakingly and meticulously going over every word and every sentence checking and rechecking the sentence structure and grammar, I would not have been able to complete it. Thank you for your ministry to me. I love you my son.

I want to thank my other children, Krista, Matt, and Kara for their love for Christ and His Word and their willingness to live for Him. I love you all.

Introduction

This workbook is designed to aid in the comprehension and application of the truths from the Scriptures which are found in the book of the same name. It has a question and answer format because asking questions was a powerful teaching method that the Lord used to reveal God's divine truth. Jesus asked over one hundred and thirty questions as He instructed the people of God and others. These are only the recorded ones. We can only speculate as to how many questions He might have actually asked. The Lord used His questioning techniques to prompt His listeners to focus, understand, analyze, evaluate, and apply the principles He was proclaiming to them. The same has been done in this workbook.

In John chapter five, through His healing ministry, the Lord Jesus had gathered a large crowd from the surrounding villages and towns who were following Him. He felt much compassion for them and viewed them as sheep without a shepherd. So, Jesus spent most of the day healing their sick and teaching them about the kingdom of God.

When late afternoon came, the Lord's disciples realized that neither they nor the large crowd that had gathered were anywhere near a place to eat. In haste, they suggested to Jesus that He send them away so they could seek sustenance in some of the surrounding villages. As the Messiah heard their concern, He saw this as a perfect opportunity to again test their faith. So, He asked a pertinent question. In John 5:5, the apostle records, "Jesus therefore lifting up his eyes, and seeing that a great multitude was coming to him, said to Philip, 'Where are we to buy bread, that these may eat?'" Philip responded first. He voiced his concern over the fact that they would need over two hundred denarii (200 days'

1

wages) to provide even a small amount of food to that large of a crowd five thousand men plus wives and children). There was no place near to buy that kind of food. And they certainly did not have the money.

Here, the Lord had the answer He sought. Though Philip viewed this as an impossible situation for man, he would discover it was something very possible for the Son of God. Jesus used the questioning process to bring to the forefront this notion that they were now in the realm of impossibility for man.

Though it would have been a powerful show of faith for Philip to have said something like, "Lord, you are the Son of God, you can do anything. Can you create food for these people?" Then, an idea popped into the head of the brother of Peter. In verse 9, Andrew speculated aloud, "There is a boy here who has five barley loaves and two fish, but what are these among so many?" He did recognize that there was some food available to share with the large crowd, but it was too little of an amount. Again, they were in an impossible situation and they had not yet realized the power that was standing in their midst.

The Lord had accomplished with His question the clear demonstration that His disciples still did not understand the greatness of His power and person. So, Jesus commanded them to have the people sit in groups of fifty or hundred all over the area. Then with a prayer of thanks to His Father, Jesus began to distribute the food from the basket of the boy. This was supernaturally created loaves and fish and it just kept coming. Finally, all were fed and satisfied. There was still enough fragments to fill twelve baskets which would be enough for the twelve disciples. As Jesus used questions, so shall we. May these questions help you focus, understand, analyze, evaluate, and apply these biblical principles.

Chapter 1

Involve God First

The first important step in the reconciliation process is the recognition that no matter who else we have sinned against, we have sinned against our God first.

In the section, "A Typical Scenario," the author describes an argument someone might have had with another that could require a reconciliation.

What is the scenario about?

What did the conflict concern?

What was the relationship between the parties?

Have you had a similar experience?

In the section, "A Scriptural Principle" the author presents an important biblical principle in the forgiveness process which concerns our sins against God in relationships.

How would you express this principle in your own words?

How would you rewrite this principle to make it even more personal to your life (using your name and situation)?

Why do you think this principle might be important in your life right now?

How would you rate yourself on the percentage of times you followed this principle in the past when you did something wrong in a relationship?

Directions: Put a horizontal mark and your name where you see yourself on the percentage line.

| 0% | 25% | 50% | 75% | 100% |

In the section, "A Biblical Explanation," the author explains the reasons why our sin is first against the Lord God when we sin against others in a relationship and what we should do about it.

In Psalm 51:4, what did King David really mean when he wrote "against you and you alone" have I sinned?

Why must the Lord God be dealt with on an "utterly divine level" when we transgress others?

According to Psalm 41:4 and 11–13, what will we experience when we confess our sins to God first?

According to Matthew 6:12 (the Lord's Prayer), what must we do before we forgive others?

According to Psalm 86:5, when we come to God and ask for forgiveness what is He ready to do?

In what ways might these truths impact your relationships?

In the section, "An Ancient Portrait," the author provides the unique portrayal of King David's sin with Bathsheba and its resultant cover-up.

What was David's sin against Uriah?

How did David attempt to cover up his sin?

How did God feel about what David had done?

What was David's response after Nathan confronted him?

Though not mentioned, what would David have needed to do once he had reconciled with God?

Have you ever been in any situation comparable to David's who attempted to cover up his sin or Uriah's who had somebody try and deceive him? How was it different? How was it the same?

In the section, "A Modern Anecdote," the author discusses a situation in which a woman's alcohol consumption reached an extreme level and the problems that occurred.

How had the wife's drinking problem escalate to the point that she needed counseling for her and her husband?

What individual responsibility did the wife and her husband bear for her difficulties with alcohol?

How did the both of them improperly handle the drinking problem?

What are two biblical reasons (with verses) why this was not the best approach?

How did the couple begin the reconciliation process using the Scriptural principle discussed in this chapter?

Based on the truths learned in this chapter, what would you have done differently if you were the wife or the husband?

In the section, "A Personal Response," the author provides a model you may use for prayer if you find it necessary after discovering the truths in this chapter.

Are you presently in a relationship where you have sinned against another and have not asked God for forgiveness? If not, is there one from the past that still needs this prayer to be prayed?

Based on the truths you have just learned, what will you continue doing in your current relationships and what will you do differently?

What additional thoughts would you like to share with the others?

Chapter 2

Leave Nothing Out

As we ask for forgiveness, we must realize God knows every detail of what we have done. So, we must confess all our wrong-doing in the relationship and hold nothing back.

In the section, "A Typical Scenario," the author describes an encounter one might have with a customer representative on the phone which may require a reconciliation.

What is the scenario about?

What did the conflict concern?

What was the relationship between the parties?

Have you had a similar experience?

In the section, "A Scriptural Principle" the author presents an important biblical principle in the forgiveness process which concerns our sin against God.

How would you express this principle in your own words?

How would you rewrite this principle to make it even more personal to your life (using your name and situation)?

Why do you think this principle might be important in your life right now?

How would you rate yourself on the percentage of times you followed this principle in the past when you did something wrong in a relationship?

Directions: Put a horizontal mark and your name where you are on the percentage line.

| 0% | 25% | 50% | 75% | 100% |

In the section, "A Biblical Explanation," the author explains the reasons why we should to own up to all our sins against others in a relationship and what we should do about it.

According to David's words in Psalm 32:3-4, and 11, what did he feel before and then after he confessed all his sins?

What are two examples (with the passages that support them) of individuals who acknowledged that God's people should confess all of their sins before Him?

In 1 Kings 8:50, what key phrase is used to indicate that Solomon was asking God to forgive every sin of His people?

In Psalm 90:8, what key phrase is used to indicate that Moses was asking God to forgive all the sins of His people?

According to Psalm 139:4 and Hebrews 4:12, how might we discover the sins we have committed in a relationship?

In what ways might these truths impact your relationships?

In the section, "An Ancient Portrait," the author provides an example of Adam and Eve committing a sin against God and their unwillingness to own up to all that they did.

When God placed Adam and Eve in the garden, what were they to do?

What was the transgression that Adam and Eve committed which destroyed their initial relationship to God?

Rather than admit all he had done, who did Adam blame?

Rather than admit all she had done, who did Eve blame?

Did God give them opportunities to admit all they had done wrong to Him?

Have you ever been in a situation that was similar to Adam and Eve's in which you or the other person blamed someone else for wrong-doing? How was it different? How was it the same?

In the section, "A Modern Anecdote," the author discusses a situation in which a husband had to own up to all the sins he committed in his sinful pornography habit before God.

How did the husband's pornography obsession negatively impact his relationship to his wife?

How did the husband feel after his wife found out?

What initial steps did the husband have to take to reconcile his relationship with God and then his wife?

Did this process come easily for the couple?

Did the wife desire to accept any responsibility for what her husband had done? Should she have? Why or why not?

Based on the truths learned in this chapter, what would you have done differently if you were husband or wife?

In the section, "A Personal Response," the author provides a model you may use for prayer if you find it necessary after discovering the truths in this chapter.

Are you presently in a relationship where you have sinned against another and have not asked God for forgiveness? If not, is there one from the past that still needs this prayer to be prayed?

Based on the truths you have just learned, what will you continue doing in your current relationships and what will you do differently?

What additional thoughts would you like to share with the others?

Chapter 3

Admit Your Sin

To restore our relationship with God, He desires us to confess our sins before Him. This is a three-fold process as we admit our sins, mourn over them, and turn from them.

In the section, "A Typical Scenario," the author describes an encounter one might have with a police officer that did not go well and may require a reconciliation.

What is the scenario about?

What did the conflict concern?

What was the relationship between the parties?

Have you had a similar experience?

In the section, "A Scriptural Principle" the author presents an important biblical principle in the forgiveness process which concerns the confession of our sins against God.

How would you express this principle in your own words?

How would you rewrite this principle to make it even more personal to your life (using your name and situation)?

Why do you think this principle might be important in your life right now?

How would you rate yourself on the percentage of times you followed this principle in the past when you did something wrong in a relationship?

Directions: Put a horizontal mark and your name where you are on the percentage line.

| 0% | 25% | 50% | 75% | 100% |

In the section, "A Biblical Explanation," the author explains the reasons why we are to fully confess all the sins against others in a relationship and how to do it.

According to 1 John 1:8, what can we never say about sin in general or in our relationships?

According to 1 John 1:9, once we realize we have sinned in a relationship what should we do?

What it the first characteristic of a repentant heart (provide a verse)?

What it the second characteristic of a truly repentant heart (provide a verse)?

What it the third characteristic of a repentant heart (provide a verse)?

In what ways might these truths impact your relationships?

In the section, "An Ancient Portrait," the author provides an devastating situation for Israel when Achan was unwilling to confess his sin before God.

What was Achan's sin against Israel?

How did Achan cover it up?

What did Joshua want Achan to do before he received his just punishment?

What qualities of repentance did Achan not demonstrate?

What was Achan's punishment and why was God so harsh?

Have you ever been in a situation comparable to Israel's in which others did not own up to their sins against you or like Achan's in which you did not take any responsibility against them? How was it different? How was it the same?

In the section, "A Modern Anecdote," the author describes an encounter with a young man who was not able to leave the home when he became an adult.

What difficulties did the mother and father have with each other that led to their son being unable to leave the home?

How was his joy with his parents much different than his joy with his friends? Why?

What unhealthy behaviors did the young man engage in to cope with the struggles of his parents?

What individual responsibility should the son have taken for his own failure to leave the home?

How did the parents and the son reconcile with each other in order for the young man to leave the home?

Based on the truths learned in this chapter, what would you have done differently if you were one of the parents or the young man?

In the section, "A Personal Response," the author provides a model you may use for prayer if you find it necessary after discovering the truths in this chapter.

Are you presently in a relationship where you have sinned against another and have not asked God for forgiveness? If not, is there one from the past that still needs this prayer to be prayed?

Based on the truths you have just learned, what will you continue doing in your current relationships and what will you do differently?

What additional thoughts would you like to share with the others?

Chapter 4

Accept God's Forgiveness

The next step is to accept God's forgiveness with a sense of blessing and gratefulness. Any sin or transgression that we could commit has already been forgiven.

In the section, "A Typical Scenario," the author describes an unpleasant dream in which one may suddenly realize all the sins he or she has committed, especially in relationships.

What is the scenario about?

What did the conflict concern?

What was the relationship between the parties?

Have you had a similar experience?

In the section, "A Scriptural Principle" the author presents an important biblical principle in the forgiveness process which concerns fully accepting God's forgiveness.

How would you express this principle in your own words?

How would you rewrite this principle to make it even more personal to your life (using your name and situation)?

Why do you think this principle might be important in your life right now?

How would you rate yourself on the percentage of times you followed this principle in the past when you did something wrong in a relationship?

Directions: Put a horizontal mark and your name where you are on the percentage line.

| 0% | 25% | 50% | 75% | 100% |

In the section, "A Biblical Explanation," the author explains the reasons why we are accept the forgiveness of God in our sins against others with a sense of blessing and gratefulness and how to do it.

According to Colossians 2:13-14, what has happened to the past sins we have committed in our relationships?

According to Hebrews 9:22, what sacrifice had to be made for our forgiveness of sins that we commit in relationships?

According to Romans 4:8 and Psalm 28:7, how should we feel about God's forgiveness of our relationship sins?

According to Hebrews 10:22, how does forgiveness compare to washing with pure water?

Does God have enough grace to forgive these sins no matter how great? How do you know (provide verse)?

In what ways might these truths impact your relationships?

In the section, "An Ancient Portrait," the author provides a picture of a woman who entered Simon's home to see Jesus. The woman repented and accepted His forgiveness with a sense of blessing and gratitude.

According to Simon, what kind of person was the woman?

Why didn't Simon understand what the woman was doing?

What three actions did the woman take to demonstrate her repentance?

What was the Lord's gracious response?

How did Simon dishonor Jesus in what he did not do?

Have you ever been in a situation similar to the woman's in which you sought forgiveness or Simon's where you may have been critical? How was it different? How was it the same?

In the section, "A Modern Anecdote," the author shares the good news with a woman who could not believe the Lord God would forgive all her sins.

What happened in the woman's life that made her feel so empty inside?

Why did the author share the gospel with her?

What does God, the Father, provide people with when they become Christians?

What held the woman back from receiving Jesus Christ as Savior and Lord?

What should the woman do if she makes more mistakes?

Based on the truths learned in this chapter, did you react in the same kind of way when you became a Christian or have you since felt this way when you sinned against another?

In the section, "A Personal Response," the author provides a model you may use for prayer if you find it necessary after discovering the truths in this chapter.

Are you presently in a relationship where you have sinned against another and have not asked God for forgiveness? If not, is there one from the past that still needs this prayer to be prayed?

Based on the truths you have just learned, what will you continue doing in your current relationships and what will you do differently?

What additional thoughts would you like to share with the others?

Chapter 5

Forgive Yourself All

Now, we must fully forgive ourselves. Though this may be difficult at times, God does not desire His children to feel guilty for their sins after confessing them.

In the section, "A Typical Scenario," the author describes an encounter with someone who had not forgiven himself for a sin he had committed in a relationship.

What is the scenario about?

What did the conflict concern?

What was the relationship between the parties?

Have you had a similar experience?

In the section, "A Scriptural Principle" the author presents an important biblical principle in the forgiveness process which concerns forgiving ourselves.

How would you express this principle in your own words?

How would you rewrite this principle to make it even more personal to your life (using your name and situation)?

Why do you think this principle might be important in your life right now?

How would you rate yourself on the percentage of times you followed this principle in the past when you did something wrong in a relationship?

Directions: Put a horizontal mark and your name where you are on the percentage line.

| 0% | 25% | 50% | 75% | 100% |

In the section, "A Biblical Explanation," the author explains the reasons why we are to forgive ourselves for the sins we commit against others in a relationship and how to do it.

According to Romans 7:20, what is inside us which keeps us from forgiving ourselves?

According to 2 Corinthians 10:5, what must we do with the false concept that our sin is too great or sins too numerous for us to forgive ourselves?

According to Romans 12:2, how can we subdue these guilt-filled thoughts that condemn?

According to Philippians 4:6–7, what must we do to guard our hearts and minds from these unforgiving thoughts?

When a memory of a sin against another returns, how are we to handle it?

In what ways might these truths impact your relationships?

In the section, "An Ancient Portrait," the author describes how Peter handled his grievous sin against the Lord and the guilt which must have accompanied it.

What was Peter's attitude when Jesus told him that he would deny him three times that night?

How did Peter actually deny Christ?

What was Peter's response after he had denied Christ?

What were the consequences of Peter's denial?

Why do you think Peter was silent about his sin in his letters (1 and 2 Peter)?

Have you ever been in a situation like Peter's in which you knew God forgave your sin against another, but you could not forgive yourself? How was it different? How was it the same?

In the section, "A Modern Anecdote," the author describes a deep struggle a husband had to forgive himself for the sin of adultery.

What did the husband mean when he said "I am that guy?"

What does a healthy fear in a relationship involve?

Why was the husband filled with anxiety?

According to Romans 7:20, where did the condemning voice inside his head come from?

What might be some safeguards the family could set up to rebuild the trust and keep this sin from occurring again?

Based on the truths learned in this chapter, how would you have reacted to your sin if you were the husband? How would you have acted if you were the wife?

In the section, "A Personal Response," the author provides a model you may use for prayer if you find it necessary after discovering the truths in this chapter.

Are you presently in a relationship where you have sinned against another and have not asked God for forgiveness? If not, is there one from the past that still needs this prayer to be prayed?

Based on the truths you have just learned, what will you continue doing in your current relationships and what will you do differently?

What additional thoughts would you like to share with the others?

Chapter 6

Ask Others Next

We constantly ask God for forgiveness and are forgiven by Him, and He desires that we do the same toward others. This pattern of confessing and forgiving is His blueprint.

In the section, "A Typical Scenario," the author describes an encounter with a father who has wrongfully accused his own daughter of denting the car and will not ask her for forgiveness.

What is the scenario about?

What did the conflict concern?

What was the relationship between the parties?

Have you had a similar experience?

In the section, "A Scriptural Principle" the author presents an important biblical principle in the forgiveness process which concerns asking others for forgiveness.

How would you express this principle in your own words?

How would you rewrite this principle to make it even more personal to your life (using your name and situation)?

Why do you think this principle might be important in your life right now?

How would you rate yourself on the percentage of times you followed this principle in the past when you did something wrong in a relationship?

Directions: Put a horizontal mark and your name where you are on the percentage line.

| 0% | 25% | 50% | 75% | 100% |

In the section, "A Biblical Explanation," the author explains the reasons why we are to ask for forgiveness when we sin against others in a relationship and how to do it.

What is the Lord God's usual pattern of dealing with sin in our relationship with Him?

According to Romans 2:15, what is inside all people which instinctively prompts them to ask others for forgiveness?

In the incident between Abimelech and Abraham, who was the one who asked for forgiveness and why?

In incident between Pharaoh and Moses, who was the one who asked for forgiveness and why?

In the incident between Nabal and David, who was the one who asked for forgiveness and why?

In what ways might these truths impact your relationships?

In the section, "An Ancient Portrait," the author describes the sin of Joseph's brothers against him and the circumstances that led them to ask him for forgiveness.

What was the brothers' sin against Joseph and why did they do it?

When Joseph met his brothers many years later, how did he demonstrate that he had already forgiven them?

What happened to make his brothers fearful that Joseph may have not forgiven them and would retaliate?

Since the brothers were fearful of facing Joseph directly, how did they ask him for forgiveness?

What was Joseph's response to their gesture?

Have you ever been in a situation that was comparable to either Joseph having to forgive a harsh sin or his brothers who needed to ask for forgiveness? How was it different? How was it the same?

In the section, "A Modern Anecdote," the author explains how two parents impulsively divorced and discovered that they had to ask for forgiveness from their children.

According to Proverbs, what was the initial step the parents had to take to resolve their divorce issues?

Why was it so important for each spouse to ask the other for forgiveness?

Why was it important for the parents ask their children for forgiveness?

How would the asking of forgiveness by the parents affect their children's future?

After the parents asked the children for forgiveness what did the children have to do and why?

Based on the truths learned in this chapter, what would you have done differently if you were one of the parents or one of the children?

In the section, "A Personal Response," the author provides a model you may use for prayer if you find it necessary after discovering the truths in this chapter.

Are you presently in a relationship where you have sinned against another and have not asked God for forgiveness? If not, is there one from the past that still needs this prayer to be prayed?

Based on the truths you have just learned, what will you continue doing in your current relationships and what will you do differently?

What additional thoughts would you like to share with the others?

Chapter 7

Humbly Make Restitution

There may be times when we should make restitution to those we have wronged. This is not a part of forgiveness on their part but a part of repentance on ours.

In the section, "A Typical Scenario," the author describes an incident where a husband and wife disagree and may need to reconcile.

What is the scenario about?

What did the conflict concern?

What was the relationship between the parties?

Have you had a similar experience?

In the section, "A Scriptural Principle" the author presents an important biblical principle in the forgiveness process which concerns making restitution toward those we have wronged.

How would you express this principle in your own words?

How would you rewrite this principle to make it even more personal to your life (using your name and situation)?

Why do you think this principle might be important in your life right now?

How would you rate yourself on the percentage of times you followed this principle in the past when you did something wrong in a relationship?

Directions: Put a horizontal mark and your name where you are on the percentage line.

| 0% | 25% | 50% | 75% | 100% |

In the section, "A Biblical Explanation," the author explains the reasons why we should demonstrate repentance through restitution when we sin against others and how to do it.

What is the relationship of restitution to our repentance and forgiveness?

According to Leviticus 6:5, how much restitution should be made and when?

According to 1 Samuel 25, how did Abigail make restitution to David for the foolishness of her husband Nabal?

What was David's response to her actions?

In what two parables is restitution presented by Jesus?

In what ways might these truths impact your relationships?

In the section, "An Ancient Portrait," the author shares the story of the salvation of Zacchaeus and his great desire to make restitution to those he had cheated.

How did tax-collectors get paid?

How did tax-collectors usually mistreat people?

What were the reactions of the people who were cheated?

When Zacchaeus believed in the Lord Jesus, what restitution did he desire to make?

How might restitution affect our relationship with those we have wronged?

Have you ever been in a situation comparable to Zacchaeus or those he wronged? How was it different? How was it the same?

In the section, "A Modern Anecdote," the author describes how a mother wronged her daughter and wanted to make restitution.

What was the mother's problem and how did she get herself into it?

What were the consequences of the mother's wrongdoing?

After her repentance, how did the mother want to make the necessary restitution?

Why did the husband want to make restitution to his wife and how was he going to do it?

Why did the daughter want to make restitution to her mom and how was she going to do it?

Based on the truths learned in this chapter, what would you have done differently if you were the husband, mother, or daughter?

In the section, "A Personal Response," the author provides a model you may use for prayer if you find it necessary after discovering the truths in this chapter.

Are you presently in a relationship where you have sinned against another and have not asked God for forgiveness? If not, is there one from the past that still needs this prayer to be prayed?

Based on the truths you have just learned, what will you continue doing in your current relationships and what will you do differently?

What additional thoughts would you like to share with the others?

Chapter 8

Accept the Consequences

When we sin in relationships, we accept the consequences as God trains us to be more like Him. These may come from God, parents, spouses, friends, bosses, churches, or the law.

In the section, "A Typical Scenario," the author describes an incident where someone forgot a task and refused to accept the consequences.

What is the scenario about?

What did the conflict concern?

What was the relationship between the parties?

Have you had a similar experience?

In the section, "A Scriptural Principle" the author presents an important biblical principle in the forgiveness process which concerns our acceptance of the consequences for our sin.

How would you express this principle in your own words?

How would you rewrite this principle to make it even more personal to your life (using your name and situation)?

Why do you think this principle might be important in your life right now?

How would you rate yourself on the percentage of times you followed this principle in the past when you did something wrong in a relationship?

Directions: Put a horizontal mark and your name where you are on the percentage line.

| 0% | 25% | 50% | 75% | 100% |

In the section, "A Biblical Explanation," the author explains the reasons why we should demonstrate repentance through accepting the consequences when we sin against others.

How is restitution related to accepting the consequences for our actions?

If someone has difficulty forgiving us, could this problem be a consequence for our wrongdoing in the relationship and why?

How does God use consequences to train us to have stronger relationships?

How would the government become involved in providing consequences for actions in a relationship?

What are two Biblical examples of God directly providing the consequences for sin?

In what ways might these truths impact your relationships?

In the section, "An Ancient Portrait," the author describes the prodigal son's desire to accept the consequences for his sin.

In what way did the younger son transgress his father and then his older brother?

How did the father respond in love?

What critical event drove the prodigal son to finally repent?

What action did the prodigal son want to take in order to accept the consequences for his sin?

Do you think the prodigal son received back all the money he had spent and why?

Have you ever been in a situation comparable to the son's desire to accept the consequences or the father's willingness to forgive?

In the section, "A Modern Anecdote," the author discusses a situation where one roommate needed to set consequences for another who was being irresponsible.

What two words might characterize the kind of relationship John and Steve had?

What did Steve do to break his relationship with John?

How did Steve display over and over his irresponsibility to John when they were growing up?

What plan did John put into place for Steve to become more responsible for his actions?

Once John had initiated the plan, what was he now free to do?

Based on the truths learned in this chapter, what would you have done differently if you were John or Steve?

In the section, "A Personal Response," the author provides a model you may use for prayer if you find it necessary after discovering the truths in this chapter.

Are you presently in a relationship where you have sinned against another and have not asked God for forgiveness? If not, is there one from the past that still needs this prayer to be prayed?

Based on the truths you have just learned, what will you continue doing in your current relationships and what will you do differently?

What additional thoughts would you like to share with the others?

Chapter 9

Gently Confront Sin

If others sin against us or we sin against them, we are to take our responsibility first for what we have done and then gently confront them.

In the section, "A Typical Scenario," the author describes an encounter between neighbors that resulted in a torn dress shirt and would require a reconciliation.

What is the scenario about?

What did the conflict concern?

What was the relationship between the parties?

Have you had a similar experience?

In the section, "A Scriptural Principle" the author presents an important biblical principle in the forgiveness process which concerns gently confronting others for their sin.

How would you express this principle in your own words?

How would you rewrite this principle to make it even more personal to your life (using your name and situation)?

Why do you think this principle might be important in your life right now?

How would you rate yourself on the percentage of times you followed this principle in the past when you did something wrong in a relationship?

Directions: Put a horizontal mark and your name where you are on the percentage line.

| 0% | 25% | 50% | 75% | 100% |

In the section, "A Biblical Explanation," the author explains the reasons why we are to gently confront those who have sinned against us in a relationship and how to do it.

What is the primary and most important purpose of gently confronting others?

In the discussion of the second and third purposes, once we know the facts, what does each party do?

The fourth purpose is to gain back your brother. What does this mean?

According to the fifth purpose, what positive result could arise from the gentle confrontation of an unbeliever?

According to the sixth purpose, what is the Devil's snare of an unbeliever that gentle confrontation can eliminate?

In what ways might these truths impact your relationships?

In the section, "An Ancient Portrait," the author describes the confrontation of the Lord Jesus by Martha concerning Mary and His response.

What was the conflict between Mary and Martha?

In what three ways did Martha improperly confront Mary?

Why had Martha become so upset about the tasks that she had taken on?

How did the Lord Jesus properly confront Martha after she had improperly confronted Him?

Why did the Lord Jesus take a stand against Martha rather than simply surrender to her demands?

Have you ever been in a situation comparable to Martha's demands, Mary's choice, or Jesus' stand and how was it the same? How was it different?

In the section, "A Modern Anecdote," the author discusses a situation in which a young woman developed unhealthy eating habits in response to her sister's criticism.

How did the young lady's eating problems begin?

How did the author immediately deal with her self-esteem problem?

Why did her older sister have to be gently confronted and what was the result?

Why did her parents have to be gently confronted and what was the result?

Why did the young lady have to be gently confronted by her parents and what was the result?

Based on the truths learned in this chapter, what would you have done differently if you were young lady who was being criticized, the older sister with all the responsibility, or the parents who were so concerned?

In the section, "A Personal Response," the author provides a model you may use for prayer if you find it necessary after discovering the truths in this chapter.

Are you presently in a relationship where you have sinned against another and have not asked God for forgiveness? If not, is there one from the past that still needs this prayer to be prayed?

Based on the truths you have just learned, what will you continue doing in your current relationships and what will you do differently?

What additional thoughts would you like to share with the others?

Chapter 10

Forgive as Forgiven

If others sin against us in a relationship, we must forgive them as God forgives us. This applies to any and all sins over the course of the relationship.

In the section, "A Typical Scenario," the author describes a co-worker stealing a Christian's idea and his unwillingness to forgive which will need reconciliation.

What is the scenario about?

What did the conflict concern?

What was the relationship between the parties?

Have you had a similar experience?

In the section, "A Scriptural Principle" the author presents an important biblical principle in the forgiveness process which concerns forgiving as we are forgiven.

How would you express this principle in your own words?

How would you rewrite this principle to make it even more personal to your life (using your name and situation)?

Why do you think this principle might be important in your life right now?

How would you rate yourself on the percentage of times you followed this principle in the past when you did something wrong in a relationship?

Directions: Put a horizontal mark and your name where you are on the percentage line.

0%	25%	50%	75%	100%

In the section, "A Biblical Explanation," the author explains the reasons why we are to forgive as we are forgiven and how to do it.

How do we sometimes make distinctions among people in our forgiveness?

According to Mark 11:25 and Luke 11:4, what key words are used by the Lord Jesus to demonstrate that all people should be forgiven whether they are believers are unbelievers?

To aid in our forgiveness process, what kind of comparison should we make concerning our own sins with the sins of those against us?

If Christians are having a difficult time of forgiving people, what might they not be doing enough of?

Is the forgiveness of others dependent on their response to us? Why or why not?

In what ways might these truths impact your relationships?

In the section, "An Ancient Portrait," the author presents the parable of the servant who was unwilling to forgive.

What was the king's response to his servant's plea?

What was the first servant's response to the second servant's plea?

How were the two responses different from each other and why?

What actions did the king take when he found out?

According to this parable of Jesus why should we forgive as forgiven?

Have you ever been in a situation comparable to the king or either servant's dilemma? How was it different or the same?

In the section, "A Modern Anecdote," the author discusses a situation in which a young lady struggled with forgiving her father.

Why did the young lady come in for counseling?

Why was the young lady bitter toward her father?

Rather than confront her father, what did she do?

How did the young lady misinterpret her father's behavior toward her mother?

Why did she not want to forgive her father?

Based on the truths learned in this chapter, what would you have done differently if you were the bitter daughter, the unknowing father, or the traditional mother?

In the section, "A Personal Response," the author provides a model you may use for prayer if you find it necessary after discovering the truths in this chapter.

Are you presently in a relationship where you have sinned against another and have not asked God for forgiveness? If not, is there one from the past that still needs this prayer to be prayed?

Based on the truths you have just learned, what will you continue doing in your current relationships and what will you do differently?

What additional thoughts would you like to share with the others?

Chapter 11

Forgive the Forgiven

When Christians struggle with forgiving other Christians who have hurt them, they should remember that God has already forgiven those very sins on the cross.

In the section, "A Typical Scenario," the author describes an angry encounter between friends which needed restoration.

What is the scenario about?

What did the conflict concern?

What was the relationship between the parties?

Have you had a similar experience?

In the section, "A Scriptural Principle" the author presents an important biblical principle in the forgiveness process which concerns forgiving the forgiven.

How would you express this principle in your own words?

How would you rewrite this principle to make it even more personal to your life (using your name and situation)?

Why do you think this principle might be important in your life right now?

How would you rate yourself on the percentage of times you followed this principle in the past when you did something wrong in a relationship?

Directions: Put a horizontal mark and your name where you are on the percentage line.

| 0% | 25% | 50% | 75% | 100% |

In the section, "A Biblical Explanation," the author explains the many reasons why we are to forgive believers who have already been forgiven by God and how to do it.

How does the Lord God's forgiveness of our sins pertain to his forgiveness of other sins against us?

According to Luke 17:3-4, is there a limit on the number of times we should forgive?

According to Matthew 26:28, what does the blood of Christ do to the sins that are committed against us by believers?

According to 1 Timothy 1:15-17, how was Paul, the apostle, the Lord's classical example of forgiveness?

Why was it so difficult for Paul to be forgiven and accepted by Christians?

In what ways might these truths impact your relationships?

In the section, "An Ancient Portrait," the author describes the parable of the Prodigal Son from the perspective of the older brother who did not want to forgive.

How did the father show the younger brother his love and forgiveness when he returned?

How did the older brother want the father to demonstrate his love to him?

Do you think the older brother loved his father and younger brother and how do you know?

What did the older brother want the father to do to the younger brother instead?

What were the three reasons why the older brother would not forgive the younger brother for what he had done?

Have you ever been in a situation comparable to the older brother who had difficulty forgiving or the father who had to handle it? How was it different? How was it the same?

In the section, "A Modern Anecdote," the author explains a son's struggle to forgive his mother who had come to Christ.

What were the three ways in which the mother traumatized the young man and his siblings growing up?

How did the man attempt to help his mother as a child?

How did the man deal with his mother once he had become an adult?

When the mother came to Christ, why did the man still have difficulty forgiving her?

What was biblical truth that caused the man to change his mind and finally forgive his mother for what she done?

Based on the truths learned in this chapter, what would you have done differently if you were the mother who neglected her children or the man who was neglected?

In the section, "A Personal Response," the author provides a model you may use for prayer if you find it necessary after discovering the truths in this chapter.

Are you presently in a relationship where you have sinned against another and have not asked God for forgiveness? If not, is there one from the past that still needs this prayer to be prayed?

Based on the truths you have just learned, what will you continue doing in your current relationships and what will you do differently?

What additional thoughts would you like to share with the others?

Chapter 12

Forgive the Lost

If Christians have difficulty with forgiving those who not know Christ, they should see them as lost in desperate need of salvation rather than as wicked in need of judgment.

In the section, "A Typical Scenario," the author contrasts the reaction of a husband with his wife's toward the mistakes of a neighbor.

What is the scenario about?

What did the conflict concern?

What was the relationship between the parties?

Have you had a similar experience?

In the section, "A Scriptural Principle" the author presents an important biblical principle in the forgiveness process which concerns viewing unbelievers as lost rather than wicked.

How would you express this principle in your own words?

How would you rewrite this principle to make it even more personal to your life (using your name and situation)?

Why do you think this principle might be important in your life right now?

How would you rate yourself on the percentage of times you followed this principle in the past when you did something wrong in a relationship?

Directions: Put a horizontal mark and your name where you are on the percentage line.

| 0% | 25% | 50% | 75% | 100% |

In the section, "A Biblical Explanation," the author explains the reasons why we are to view unbelievers as lost in order to forgive them and how to do it.

In Luke 9:51–56, what did James and John want to do to the Samaritan village for rejecting Jesus and what was the Lord's response?

How is the concept of man being lost and blind related?

If those who sin against us receive Christ, what will happen to those sins?

What are two groups who participated in Christ's crucifixion and how did He view them in order to forgive them?

Though Christ asked God, the Father, to forgive them, could they be forgiven without receiving Christ? Why or why not?

In what ways might these truths impact your relationships?

In the section, "An Ancient Portrait," the author portrays the struggle of the prophet Jonah to obey God's command.

Why did Jonah run when commanded to preach the gospel to the Ninevites and what was God's response?

After the storm came, what did the ship's crew finally decide to do with Jonah when they discovered it was his fault?

After sometime in the belly of the great fish, why did Jonah finally repent?

What contradiction in the Prophet Jonah's thinking led him to be hypocrite when it came to God's mercy?

What was the response of the Ninevites to Jonah's message and what does this tell us about God?

Have you ever been in any situation comparable to Jonah's wicked perspective or the Ninevite's desperation? How was it different? How was it the same?

In the section, "A Modern Anecdote," the author describes a man angry and bitter against his father and how he learned to forgive him.

Why was the son so angry and bitter against his father?

How did the son demonstrate his bitterness?

Was the father a Christian, why or why not?

How did the believing son need to view his father in order to fully forgive him?

Since the father had passed away, how should the son finally decide to outwardly demonstrate his forgiveness?

Based on the truths learned in this chapter, what would you have done differently if you were the son who was neglected or the father who did the neglecting?

In the section, "A Personal Response," the author provides a model you may use for prayer if you find it necessary after discovering the truths in this chapter.

Are you presently in a relationship where you have sinned against another and have not asked God for forgiveness? If not, is there one from the past that still needs this prayer to be prayed?

Based on the truths you have just learned, what will you continue doing in your current relationships and what will you do differently?

What additional thoughts would you like to share with the others?

Chapter 13

Keep No Records

To fully forgive others means not only forgiving but also forgetting. We should not to keep records of past offenses in order to punish others over and over.

In the section, "A Typical Scenario," the author describes a man's harshly reminding his wife of her past mistakes which will require a reconciliation.

What is the scenario about?

What did the conflict concern?

What was the relationship between the parties?

Have you had a similar experience?

In the section, "A Scriptural Principle" the author presents an important biblical principle in the forgiveness process which concerns forgiving and then forgetting the offenses.

How would you express this principle in your own words?

How would you rewrite this principle to make it even more personal to your life (using your name and situation)?

Why do you think this principle might be important in your life right now?

How would you rate yourself on the percentage of times you followed this principle in the past when you did something wrong in a relationship?

Directions: Put a horizontal mark and your name where you are on the percentage line.

| 0% | 25% | 50% | 75% | 100% |

In the section, "A Biblical Explanation," the author explains the reasons why we should never keep records of the sins others have committed against us and how to do it.

What does the "churning" over and over others' sins against us result in?

When the Bible says "keep no records," what two things does it involve? What does it not involve?

What can happen to our relationships if we constantly bring up the sins of the past?

In 2 Corinthians 2:7, what was Paul's response when church members kept bringing up the repentant man's offense?

Does our Father, God, bring up our transgressions against Him over and over? Why or why not?

In what ways might these truths impact your relationships?

In the section, "An Ancient Portrait," the author describes the how Jesus did not hold Martha's previous sin against her when she confronted Him about allowing Lazarus to die.

What happened the first time Martha confronted the Lord?

After receiving a message from Martha, why did Jesus wait two more days before he began the journey to Lazarus?

When Martha chastised the Lord for not arriving in time, how did Jesus respond? How could He have?

When Mary took the same approach to Jesus as her sister, how did Jesus respond? How could He have responded?

Why didn't Jesus hold the previous confrontation against the sisters and refuse to resurrect Lazarus from the dead?

Have you ever been in a situation comparable to the Lord's second chastisement or Martha's constant confrontation? How was it different? How was it the same?

In the section, "A Modern Anecdote," the author shares the deep struggle of a daughter with her mother's reminders of her past mistakes.

What three transgressions of the daughter was on the list of her mother's mental records of sins against her?

How did the harsh reminders impact the daughter?

When the mother was gently confronted about what she had done, what was her initial reaction?

What was the mother's final response?

What was the next step the mother had to take after this final response?

Based on the truths learned in this chapter, what would you have done differently if you were the record-keeping mother or the discouraged daughter?

In the section, "A Personal Response," the author provides a model you may use for prayer if you find it necessary after discovering the truths in this chapter.

Are you presently in a relationship where you have sinned against another and have not asked God for forgiveness? If not, is there one from the past that still needs this prayer to be prayed?

Based on the truths you have just learned, what will you continue doing in your current relationships and what will you do differently?

What additional thoughts would you like to share with the others?

Chapter 14

Restore Through Action

Once our sins have been dealt with through forgiveness, we begin the restoration process. This will involve a change in our words and actions allowing the feelings to follow.

In the section, "A Typical Scenario," the author describes a broken relationship between a man and his mother which needed reconciliation.

What is the scenario about?

What did the conflict concern?

What was the relationship between the parties?

Have you had a similar experience?

In the section, "A Scriptural Principle" the author presents an important biblical principle in the forgiveness process which concerns the restoring of relationships through action.

How would you express this principle in your own words?

How would you rewrite this principle to make it even more personal to your life (using your name and situation)?

Why do you think this principle might be important in your life right now?

How would you rate yourself on the percentage of times you followed this principle in the past when you did something wrong in a relationship?

Directions: Put a horizontal mark and your name where you are on the percentage line.

| 0% | 25% | 50% | 75% | 100% |

In the section, "A Biblical Explanation," the author explains the reasons why we must restore the relationship through actions and how to do it.

What is the first step in mending a broken relationship?

In the second step of the mending process, what should we remind ourselves of?

In the third step of this process, what kind of actions should be taken?

As we mend the holes in our relationships, should we focus on our feelings? Why or why not?

According to Galatians 6:1, who should start the restoration process?

In what ways might these truths impact your relationships?

In the section, "An Ancient Portrait," the author describes Jacob's reconciliation with Esau.

What was the initial problem between Jacob and Esau which caused the rift in their relationship?

Why did Jacob have to finally face Esau? Do you think God was behind this and why?

What steps did Jacob take to reconcile with his brother?

How did Esau respond?

Did the brothers become close after this restoration? Why or why not?

Have you ever been in any situation comparable to Jacob's deceit or Esau's contempt and yet have to face the other person? How was it different? How was it the same?

In the section, "A Modern Anecdote," the author explains the difficulties a set of triplets were experiencing with each other and how they were able to reconcile.

How did these siblings handle their conflicts while growing up?

How did the mother respond?

When the triplets became adults, how did they handle the family interactions?

Why was it important for the children of the triplets to have their parents reconcile?

When did some feelings of love for one another finally begin to appear?

Based on the truths learned in this chapter, what would you have done differently if you were one of the triplets or the mother?

In the section, "A Personal Response," the author provides a model you may use for prayer if you find it necessary after discovering the truths in this chapter.

Are you presently in a relationship where you have sinned against another and have not asked God for forgiveness? If not, is there one from the past that still needs this prayer to be prayed?

Based on the truths you have just learned, what will you continue doing in your current relationships and what will you do differently?

What additional thoughts would you like to share with the others?

Conclusion

As we conclude this book, I would like to leave us with some final thoughts about our God of forgiveness and what His Son did on the cross for us. First, if we understand the full extent of what was wrought for us on that cursed tree in order to forgive us, it will become so much easier to do the same thing for others. Second, if you read this entire book and realized that you do not understand salvation or have never received Christ as Lord and Savior, then I would like to provide that opportunity. Please do not skip this section; it may be the most important in your life.

From all outward appearances, humans seem "good" and attempt to live decent lives. This is man's concept of himself. This is not God's concept. The Almighty's view is that people all over the world and throughout the ages sin, sin, and sin again (Romans 3:23). This is a terrible and utterly destructive condition. Yet, they have ramifications that are far worse. These sins condemn us to everlasting divine retribution.

Though described briefly in the Old Testament, the Lord Jesus Christ clearly announced and proclaimed the future punishment to come. Contrary to popular belief, Jesus did not only speak of love, grace, and mercy, He also spoke of the coming judgment for sin. He declared that the judgment of sin would be everlasting punishment in a place He called "Hell." The Lord portrayed this place as an eternal inferno (Matthew 18:8) where there would be the weeping (from the sorrow) and gnashing of teeth (from the agony and anguish of suffering) continually into eternity (Matthew 8:12; 13:42, 50; 22:13; 24:51; 25:30; Luke 13:28).

Why must people face this horrific punishment? Though God is a God of love, grace, and mercy, He is also a God of great holiness, righteousness, and justice (Psalm 89:14,18). These attributes are just as much a part of His divine nature as His love, grace, and mercy. You have broken God's law as we all have and the penalty must be paid. This began with the first man Adam (Genesis 3:1-7). When this occurred, His love, grace, and mercy surfaced and a provision was made. Someone else would have to take man's place and pay the penalty. Someone who had never transgressed Him, who would never deserve punishment, and would fulfill all of God's Laws, would be substituted in man's place. This was the Son of God, Jesus Christ.

As the God-Man, He would pay the penalty for our sins in His death on the cross. Once done, the Lord God made only one provision for people to appropriate what His Son had done on the cross for them. This provision is receiving Jesus Christ as Savior and Lord. Though I cannot possibly share with you this good news in the confines of this book, I would love for you to consider purchasing my book entitled, *Finding The Light: The Kingdom of Heaven and How To Enter It.* It can be found for sale on Amazon.com. It is inexpensive and contains the full gospel message for your consideration. This message is so important and extensive that it cannot adequately be contained in a few pages at the end of a book.

If you are a believer, you must go out into the world and forgive as you are forgiven. These principles are to be lived and shared with others. You now have the tools to make your relationships last a lifetime. Go live them out and share them with others!

ABOUT THE AUTHOR

Dr. Donald Jones is currently a Christian Pastoral Counselor with thirty-eight years of experience in the fields of pastoral ministry, public education, and Christian counseling. He carries degrees and certificates from four major universities and from a variety of educational institutions. He has been a professor of Languages and Bible, a television commentator, and a featured speaker at a variety of events and seminars at churches, schools, and other organizations across the United States. He is a member in good standing of several secular and Christian professional organizations. Dr. Jones has been a published author since 1976. For further information view his website at www.donjonesphd.com.

www.ingramcontent.com/pod-product-compliance
Lightning Source LLC
Chambersburg PA
CBHW021208020426
42331CB00003B/257